D0576925

PRESENTED TO:

_____

FROM:

_____

DATE:

_____

A STANDARD OF

guided journal

EMILY LEY

THOMAS NELSON
Since 1798

A Standard of Grace

© 2018 Emily Ley

All rights reserved. No portion of this book may be reproduced, stored in a retrieval system, or transmitted in any form or by any means—electronic, mechanical, photocopy, recording, scanning, or other—except for brief quotations in critical reviews or articles, without the prior written permission of the publisher.

Published in Nashville, Tennessee, by Thomas Nelson. Thomas Nelson is a registered trademark of HarperCollins Christian Publishing, Inc.

Published in association with Folio Literary Management LLC, 630 Ninth Avenue, Suite 1101, New York, New York 10036.

Photography by Gina Zeidler, Tiffany McClure, Sara Coffin, and Laura Foote

Thomas Nelson titles may be purchased in bulk for educational, business, fund-raising, or sales promotional use. For information, please e-mail SpecialMarkets@ThomasNelson.com.

Unless otherwise noted, Scripture quotations are taken from the Holy Bible, New International Version®, NIV®. Copyright © 1973, 1978, 1984, 2011 by Biblica, Inc.® Used by permission of Zondervan. All rights reserved worldwide. www.Zondervan.com. The "NIV" and "New International Version" are trademarks registered in the United States Patent and Trademark Office by Biblica, Inc.®

Scripture quotations marked CEV are from the Contemporary English Version. Copyright © 1991, 1992, 1995 by American Bible Society. Used by permission.

Scripture quotations marked MSG are from *The Message*. Copyright © by Eugene H. Peterson 1993, 1994, 1995, 1996, 2000, 2001, 2002. Used by permission of Tyndale House Publishers, Inc.

Scripture quotations marked NKJV are from the New King James Version®. © 1982 by Thomas Nelson. Used by permission. All rights reserved.

Scripture quotations marked NLT are from the *Holy Bible*, New Living Translation. © 1996, 2004, 2007, 2013, 2015 by Tyndale House Foundation. Used by permission of Tyndale House Publishers, Inc., Carol Stream, Illinois 60188. All rights reserved.

Any Internet addresses, phone numbers, or company or product information printed in this book are offered as a resource and are not intended in any way to be or to imply an endorsement by Thomas Nelson, nor does Thomas Nelson vouch for the existence, content, or services of these sites, phone numbers, companies, or products beyond the life of this book.

ISBN-13: 978-1-4041-0851-6 (custom)

Printed in China

18 19 20 21 22 23 HaHa 10 9 8 7 6 5 4 3 2 1

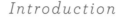

FREE FOR ALL

Hi, friends!

Here's the thing about grace: you don't have to be perfect to embrace it. Grace is *free*—for imperfect and unworthy people like you and me. Did you catch that? You don't have to be perfect! I don't either! While we are busy trying to plan extravagant birthday parties and have exquisitely put-together homes, God has set a standard totally outside our realm of thinking. Instead of calling us to be hopeless overachievers, He calls us to "walk by the Spirit . . . [with] love, joy, peace, forbearance, kindness, goodness, faithfulness, gentleness and self-control" (Galatians 5:16, 22–23). Nowhere in there did He mention perfect get-togethers, size 4 jeans, home-cooked dinners, or spotless homes.

God is pouring grace on us every day, abundantly and without restraint. So, sister, if God is giving us so much grace, why on earth aren't we having a little more grace with ourselves? Why are we running ourselves ragged trying to measure up? This rat race of ours exhausting. And it's really easy to feel like a hamster in a wheel chasing an impossible glossy-magazine standard we've set for ourselves. Grace, and only grace, offers us a way to step off that wheel—a deep breath, a place to rest, and the opportunity to slow down and savor what truly matters.

This journey to grace is just that . . . a journey, complete with stops and starts and times when you'll want to circle back and revisit a particular spot. For that reason, this journal includes multiple ribbons so that you can return to certain thoughts as you learn to embrace yourself, your life, your people in grace.

emily

ABUNDANT GRACE

"I have come that they may have life, and that
they may have it more abundantly."

—JOHN 10:10 NKJV

God cares about us abiding by His commandments and loving big—feeling deeply alive and free from the traps of perfection and comparison. He's watching us scurry about, saying, "Sweet girls, why are you so hard on yourselves? All this worry and busyness is for what? I've given you all you need."

Where did you get the idea that you had to be "put together" in every area of your life? Who defined perfection for you?

Perfect doesn't
equal worthy.

In the space below, write a description of the standard you're holding yourself to. What do you expect of yourself on a daily basis?

I WILL HOLD MYSELF TO A STANDARD OF GRACE, NOT PERFECTION.

2

HEART-BURSTING JOY

"Ask and you will receive, and your joy will be complete."

—JOHN 16:24

Somewhere between three and fortysomething we lost our joy. And now we're all trying to find it again. Our grown-up circumstances, mortgages, taxes, jobs, and social media comparison have sucked the wind right out of our sails. And here we are, convinced that getting down to our college weight and maintaining a spotless home sounds like a pretty good way to be unabashedly happy again. The truth is, if we take care of ourselves the same way we're nurturing everyone else, we'll find all sorts of joy and be better for everyone we love.

Describe what extravagant joy looks like to you. What would it take to bring back the type of heart-bursting joy you may have felt as a little child?

> Here's the thing about doing it all: even if you can do it all, no one can do it all **WELL**.

When was the last time you were ecstatically happy?

3

A VESSEL OF LOVE

*The entire law is fulfilled in keeping this one
command: "Love your neighbor as yourself."*

—GALATIANS 5:14

You have a lot going on. You want to be everything to everyone, so you're running on empty, even though you know better. How do you even begin to have grace with yourself in these situations? It all comes down to this question: What good are you when you're overwhelmed, overbooked, and overcommitted?

You are a living, breathing vessel of love. You need care, rest, nutrients, and a full heart to be able to speak life into the people you love.

How are you? Seriously . . .

What would it look like if you cared for yourself as well as you cared for others in your life? First list the things you do for others. Then list the things you do for yourself.

You may be bending over backward to give your loved ones a good life, but if you're not taking care of yourself too, you're moving backward— away from that goal.

THE GOOD STUFF

For everything there is a season.

—ECCLESIASTES 3:1 NLT

In their final moments, most people think back to big family dinners and moments with dear friends. They speak sincere, heartfelt words of love and life to their family members. They marvel over the good stuff, the memories made in the margin—not their biggest accomplishments.

This realization gives a new perspective on life, one of gratitude and immediacy. When our time becomes short, our priorities are suddenly jolted into place. I don't know about you, but this makes some of what I fill my days with seem very trivial and unimportant.

What if we lived every day with this kind of perspective? How would you be unapologetic about your priorities in a genuine, heartfelt way?

How would you pour love into your people and speak truth and
encouragement without concern about their response?

_____

_____

_____

_____

_____

_____

Who says
you have to
be so busy all
the time?

_____

_____

_____

PERMISSION TO SLOW DOWN

When I said, "My foot is slipping,"
*your unfailing love, L*ORD*, supported me.*
When anxiety was great within me,
your consolation brought me joy.

PSALM 94:18-19

When we are desperately worried, we often point our focus inward, robbing ourselves of faith and weakening our hearts. When we are weak, we aren't our best selves. We can't draw water from an empty well. And when we are empty, we're good for no one.

You may be thinking, *I'm in it. How do I get out?* The answer is this: give yourself permission to slow down. In fact, give yourself permission to just stop. Press pause on as much as possible, and take inventory of your life.

What are your commitments and responsibilities?

You get **OUT**
what you
put **IN.**

Now make a short list of your priorities. Based on that list, what can go? What can you say no to?

Give yourself permission
to **SLOW DOWN**.

BE STILL

"Be still, and know that I am God."

—PSALM 46:10

For years, I've struggled to find ways to make the good stuff the priority and let the extra commitments happen as they may, rather than the other way around. Making margin in our days means clearing room in our schedule to slow down, but it also means choosing to be still even when tasks need to be completed. The magic is that when I think about extra commitments as secondary to the good stuff, tasks start to fall away naturally and people become the most important. The have-tos are still important, but they're less of a nuisance.

Take a look at your calendar. What commitments aren't absolutely essential to the function of your family? What commitments steal margin from your days instead of bringing value to them?

_____

_____

_____

_____

_____

_____

_____

_____

_____

_____

_____

_____

What would you do with the white space in your days? Where would you be still, and which moments would you savor?

> The peace of contentment is just as valuable as the confetti that comes with achievement.

CULTIVATE CONTENTMENT

CONTENTMENT: *a state of happiness and satisfaction*

—MERRIAM-WEBSTER'S DICTIONARY

There's more to life than the hustle and bustle. We want to feel deeply alive, to make a big impact, to chase enormous dreams, to invest in what matters most. And in the midst of all of this, one challenge rises to the surface: *contentment*. This is a difficult concept for many overachieving perfectionists. But what would it look like to make room in your heart, home, and life for God to speak more clearly?

Where do you see yourself overconsuming?

> Ultimately, simplifying allows us to slow down enough to savor this life.

Keep track of your spending over the next week, and meditate on the items you waste the most on. What hole might you be trying to fill?

By **SIMPLIFYING** our lives, we're making space for what matters—to hear God more clearly, to give more wholeheartedly, and to place our energy in people and hearts rather than in things.

What would a "contentment challenge" look like for you? Be unflinchingly honest.

CHOOSING THE GOOD
OVER THE PERFECT

*"Mary has chosen what is better, and it
will not be taken away from her."*

—LUKE 10:42

Our kitchens may not be spotless, but the drips of ice cream came from an impromptu late-night sundae party, so we happily wipe them up. We may not have been on a fancy date in three years, but we've enjoyed many a good conversation on the front porch, holding hands and counting our blessings. Our floors may be covered with crumbs, but the mess is worth being able to savor the scramble.

Amid the scramble, we can do things to make the savoring a little easier.
Think about how you can you implement some of these tools:

DECLUTTER DISTRACTIONS. *Take inventory of your life, rigorously eliminate distractions, remove the unnecessary, and pare down to what truly matters.*

PUT TOOLS IN PLACE. *Set up accountability, systems, and resources.*

Life may be messy, but the mess is worth it.

ESTABLISH ROUTINES THAT WORK. *Create flexible routines so all parts of your life work together rather than competeing for time and attention.*

LIVING WITH INTENTION

Those who are wise will find a time and a way to do what is right.

—ECCLESIASTES 8:5 NLT

At certain times in life, our calendars are slam full. We're working our fingers to the bone to keep food on the table and are stretched thin, with no relief in sight. Even in those times, being intentional with our time is key to finding joy. Every yes we say is a choice to say no to something that is a lower priority.

Make a list of everything fighting for your attention—clubs, schools, sports, volunteer organizations, committees, work—everything.

Now cross out the ones that can go. Take ten minutes and quit.

However you do it, give yourself the gift of margin. Start with self-reflection, and then make sure your calendar reflects your intention.

SURRENDERING CONTROL

Many are the plans in a person's heart, but
it is LORD's purpose that prevails.

PROVERBS 19:21

So often, we think we know what's best for our lives. We plan; we strive;
we try to be in charge. But the reality is that we're not in control! This need
to be in control, to orchestrate the perfect scenario for every journey of our
lives, only breeds anxiety in our hearts.

Which imperfect puzzle are you trying to put together right now? Where do you need to let go?

So many times I've shaken my fists at God and told Him that if He'd just listen to me, He'd see that my plan is really, really good.

What worries are you stockpiling? List them here. Which worry can you release today?

11

LETTING GO

See, God has come to save me.
I will trust in him and not be afraid.
The LORD GOD is my strength and my song;
he has given me victory.

—ISAIAH 12:2 NLT

We try to do the right things, eat the right things, and say the right things to get the results we hope for. Our inability to trust that it will be okay, even if all the pieces don't fit just right, can lead to comparison, worry, and unhappiness. Sometimes greater gladness can be found in the mess than if everything had gone "according to plan." And guess what? It's okay to let go.

TIPS FOR LETTING GO

Identify those areas of your life where you're holding tightly to the reins.

The joy is in the journey, even the hard journeys.

Think through the worst-case scenario if you loosen your grip and give in to the mess or the unknown a bit. What does it look like?

Finally, give yourself some grace. You're doing a good job! Perfect isn't always best.

GRACE WITH YOURSELF

"But blessed is the one who trusts in the Lord,
whose confidence is in him.
They will be like a tree planted by the water."

—JEREMIAH 17:7–8

Your body is a vessel of love, and your heart is a well. Neglect yourself, and your heart will run dry. Care for yourself, as you would a loved one, and your heart will brim with the good stuff of life: patience, love, kindness, and empathy. Perfection is overrated. There is joy in the mess, the circus, and the seventh load of laundry if you allow yourself to be still enough to see it.

What makes you feel refreshed? Curling up with a good book? Going for a walk? List those things here.

_____

_____

_____

_____

_____

_____

_____

> Grace is an outstretched hand, ready to deliver you from the hamster wheel of trying to do it all.

_____

_____

_____

How could you rearrange your day to give yourself thirty minutes of grace and refreshment—just for you?

_____

_____

_____

_____

_____

_____

_____

In those moments when we give ourselves the grace to let everything else fall away, we find our most sincere happiness.

PRIORITIZING YOU

Fix your thoughts on what is true, and honorable, and right, and pure, and lovely, and admirable. Think about things that are excellent and worthy of praise.

—PHILIPPIANS 4:8 NLT

Most women constantly pour into others—their children, their spouses, their work, their friends. How can you nurture yourself the way you nurture and help others? Begin with this simple task: fill your well with goodness, such as joy, happiness, play, laughter, creativity, and fresh air. I can't find a single thing draining about any of those things. While feeling overwhelmed, anxiety, and stress drain the well, these nurturing activities fill it back up.

Make a list of the things that bring you joy, happiness, and laughter. What brings out your playful side? Your creative side?

You get to decide whether you will live your life insanely busy or embrace simplicity, make active changes, and slow down.

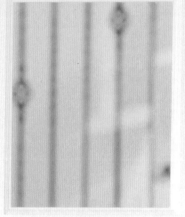
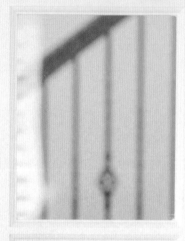

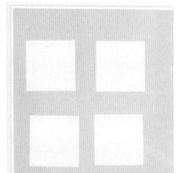

YOU HAVE PERMISSION
TO MAKE YOURSELF
A PRIORITY.

Create a plan not only to carve out a time each week to explore these things, but also to incorporate them into your everyday moments.

GRACE WITH YOUR PEOPLE

Since God chose you to be the holy people he loves,
you must clothe yourselves with tenderhearted mercy,
kindness, humility, gentleness, and patience.

—COLOSSIANS 3:12 NLT

Isn't it amazing that God doesn't make us do this life alone? He gives us people—spouses, siblings, friends, parents, children—and we have incalculable influence on those lives. As perfectly imperfect human beings, we're constantly impacting and affecting other people. What a great responsibility. When we keep that in mind, simple conversations and passing interactions begin to carry weight.

When life feels crazy, it's sometimes easy to forget the gift of the people placed in our lives. Who are your people? What are your favorite things about them?

What could you do to deepen your relationships with these people?

God's **GRACE** shines through
our ability to love others with sincere
patience, gratitude, and acceptance.

GRACE IN THE CIRCUS

*Let us come boldly to the throne of our gracious
God. There we will receive his mercy, and we will
find grace to help us when we need it most.*

—HEBREWS 4:16 NLT

No matter what season you're in, life can get more than a little crazy.
Some weeks, max capacity can feel like a daily occurrence. I've come to
realize that sometimes joining the circus is better than trying to tame it.

Make a list of five messes or tasks that you are continually struggling to tackle. Beside each mess, list a sweeter activity that will give you time with those you love. Give yourself permission to make that choice at least once this week.

If we don't intentionally **SLOW** down, this precious, messy season will **PASS** us by.

We're all better off
settling into the
circus—learning how
to be comfortable
in the sideshow.

16

THE *REAL* GOOD LIFE

See what great love the Father has lavished on us, that we should be called children of God! And that is what we are!

—1 JOHN 3:1

Somewhere along the way, the world told you that you weren't good enough. Not the way you are. Forget that. Forget what the world is telling you. You don't have to constantly strive to be more. You are enough. You deserve simple, slow, and sweet. You are worthy of happiness. You deserve silly, extravagant joy, belly laughs, and rich memories worthy of being slowly retold in rocking chairs on front porches. This is attainable—where you are, as you are, with what you have right now. You just need grace.

What does your real "good life" look like—the life you've been longing for? The one that's simple, slow, and sweet?

True joy isn't found in having it all together.

All those flaws you see in yourself and in your life . . . How can you begin giving yourself the grace to see them as simply being real?

THE GOOD LIFE IS
RICH, SLOW, REAL,
AND FLAWED.

17

BREATHE IN GRACE

"Slow down. Take a deep breath. What's the hurry?
Why wear yourself out? Just what are you after anyway?"

—JEREMIAH 2:25 MSG

Another lie you have been told is that you have to do it all—and that you have to do it all by yourself. So instead of saying no, paring down, and embracing quality of life over quantity of commitments, you have allowed your life to spin out of control. And it's left you without half a second to take a deep breath.

Take a minute. A long minute even.

Breathe in.

Breathe out.

Our society glorifies busyness and champions the adrenaline rush. But you don't have to.

Is chasing perfection your way of searching for joy? What would really happen if you said, "I'm done trying to be everything to everyone"?

> Being perfect isn't really all it's cracked up to be; real life is so much richer.

We believe we're doing the selfless thing, but we eventually self-sabotage by not investing time in ourselves.

What if you exchanged that impossible standard you've been holding yourself to for a standard of grace?

18

DEEPLY ALIVE

"Those who drink the water I give will never be thirsty again. It becomes a fresh, bubbling spring within them, giving them eternal life."

—JOHN 4:14 NLT

What would your life look like if you let your well be filled, even five minutes a day, with the things that make you feel deeply alive? It's not as hard as it seems to infuse your life with tiny moments of joy that will soon add up to a spiritual shift. Wake up twenty minutes early to savor your favorite dark-roast coffee with hazelnut cream. Put pictures of your last beach trip on your desk. Ditch the dirty kitchen counter tonight for five minutes of rocking-chair time. You get out what you put in.

List the things you love.

I love . . .

Why, oh why, are we not filling our free time with all the good things?

Looking at your list, what is your life missing? What is it you need to make you feel deeply alive? And how can you fill your heart up with that, even if just a tiny bit?

INVEST IN YOURSELF.

19

MOMENTS TO SAVOR

Teach us to live well!
Teach us to live wisely and well!

—PSALM 90:12 MSG

What we spend our time on so often indicates what we value. But so many of us have the same calendar problem: when we squeeze appointment after meeting after errand onto our schedules, we edge out time for joy. We tell the savorable moments of joy, "I just don't have time for you. But I sure do have time for committees and Facebook and folding clothes."

When did we decide that we weren't a good mom/wife/friend/daughter/professional if we didn't pack the calendar to maximum capacity? Isn't it time to give ourselves the grace—and permission—to reevaluate?

Are you ready to reevaluate? To make room for "savorable moments of joy"?

MAKE MARGIN FOR WHAT MATTERS.

be
still...

What do you really want your days to look like, to be filled with? What steps do you need to take to make it happen?

The battle for our hearts is won when we strip our schedules down to the raw essentials—the things that truly fire us up.

20

MAX CAPACITY

*"Take my yoke upon you and learn from me, for I am gentle
and humble in heart, and you will find rest for your souls."*

—MATTHEW 11:29

There is a concrete limit to how much you can fit in your brain and how much your body can handle. At some point, when there is too much for you to remember or worry about or think through, you start to forget things. Tasks fall through the cracks. Because you're overwhelmed, over-booked, overcommitted, and overstressed.

A common reaction is to feel guilty, or like you're failing in some way. Not so! This is simple cause and effect: you have limits, and you have them for a reason. And friend, you do not have to drive yourself like a beast of burden to go beyond your capacity.

Why do we drive ourselves to keep going and doing? What is so often the end result?

White space in
your calendar is
priceless. Why
work so hard
to fill it up?

We can construct our schedules in a way that allows us to truly savor the good stuff in between the have-tos of life. What are the things you long to savor?

It's the in-between moments where we find the most joy.

21

CAPTAIN MODE

We plan the way we want to live,
but only God makes us able to live it.

—PROVERBS 16:9 MSG

In our quest to have keep everything under our control, we often steal the wheel from God. We're in Captain Mode as we try to steer ourselves out of disaster and into perfection. The result? We end up driving ourselves straight into a wall. Head-on. Crash and burn.

Don't fall for the lie that if you work hard enough at keeping it all together, you'll get there. Give yourself the grace of letting God have control.

Do you struggle with putting all your hope and trust in your own hands? In what areas is this most tempting to do?

Captain Mode: I've got this. I can do this alone. I will save the day and steer the ship.

Worry, anxiety, the need for control, and the chase of perfection zap the life,
energy, and health from our bodies. How might saying no, letting go, and
letting God handle the rest make you a healthier person, not just physically,
but mentally and spiritually as well?

As busy, task-
oriented, ambitious
women, we so often
want to steer our
own courses toward
our ideal lives.

22

CHASING JOY

Even though you do not see him now, you believe in him and
are filled with an inexpressible and glorious joy, for you are
receiving the end result of your faith, the salvation of your souls.

—1 PETER 1:8–9

We're all chasing joy. Some joy comes when you least expect it. And some joy comes because you set yourself up for it. So how do you tactically set yourself up for joy? It starts with grace, continues with a plan, and ends with grace.

When you make a plan, wrap it up in a giant hug of grace, because it may not happen, or it may not happen the way you intended. Let go of the perfect plan, and pursue a good and flexible plan—one that will give you the freedom to go with the flow and find the joy hidden in the in-between moments.

What are the things that matter most to you? Are they things like dinnertime conversations, evening walks in the neighborhood, and actual face time with the people you love?

Choose to create opportunities for joy.

How can you carve out space for those things that matter most? How can you catch that joy you've been chasing?

Outer order contributes to inner calm.

—GRETCHEN RUBIN

THE GRACE TO STEP AWAY

Open your mouth and taste, open your
eyes and see—how good God is.

—PSALM 34:8 MSG

It's okay to step away. To give yourself permission to give in to the mess. When life becomes overwhelming, let the good stuff win. When juggling all the responsibilities gets to be too much, put the laptop away and go stomp in some mud puddles. When laundry mounts and housework screams your name, leave the madness behind and head to the park. Sometimes, the way to step off the hamster wheel is to literally step away from the stressor. And in those messy moments, you just might find your realest self.

Is it hard for you to step away? How can you reframe your thoughts—and then
your actions—to choose the good life?

It's okay to be
a quitter when
you're choosing
what matters.

Do you believe a clean house equals a happy home? Would occasionally choosing the mess make for more happiness?

The hamster wheel of trying to do it all is an exhausting place to be.

THE BALANCING ACT

*"Seek first his kingdom and his righteousness, and
all these things will be given to you as well."*

—MATTHEW 6:33

You've heard the term *balancing act*, right? I'm convinced that the idea of balance in life isn't a real thing. It's basically a balancing *act*. No one actually achieves it. Instead, God continually pulls us to and fro, and we have to flow with the changing situation. It's like riding a bike: we're never really perfectly perched on that seat. We're constantly shifting our weight from side to side to keep from face-planting. We could say we're balanced on the bike, but we're really in a state of continuous movement and compensation.

Over time, I've developed a few nonnegotiables that keep my priorities in check and keep me upright on the proverbial bike of life. They make decision-making simpler when the day gets crazy.

1. Family comes first. Period.

2. My work is my ministry. If it becomes too teary, too difficult to manage, and too off-kilter, it's time to reevaluate.

3. I will be fiercely and unapologetically dedicated to what matters. On top of my short list of what matters: my people.

Create your own set of life rules. What are your nonnegotiables?

1.
_____

_____

_____

_____

_____

_____

_____

_____

2.
_____

_____

_____

3.

Instead of striving for balance in your life, work toward a life fiercely devoted to what matters.

25

YOUR GRACE SPACE

As for me and my family, we will serve the Lord.

—JOSHUA 24:15 NLT

Your physical space has an enormous impact on your happiness. The things you fill your home with can either distract you or inspire you. By devoting some attention to organizing your time, your stuff, and your environment, you can make room for that happiness and inspiration.

Your happiness by no means depends on things being clean and tidy. Thinking that way is like hopping a fast train to Anxietyville, and it's just plain not real life. But remember: you are in charge of your space, and your space is a tool. Wield that tool to your advantage. Make your home your grace space.

What sort of place do you want your home to be—for yourself, for family, for friends?

> You don't need a Pinterest-perfect home; you need a home that works for you and makes you feel alive.

You need a
space, fancy
or not, that
allows you to be
your best self.

BLESS
THIS
MESS.

As you go through the next few days, jot down the things about your home and the way you live in it that work, as well as those that don't work. Look for ways to make your space work for you.

26

FINDING GRACE IN CONTENTMENT

Keep your lives free from the love of money and be
content with what you have, because God has said,
"Never will I leave you; never will I forsake you."

—HEBREWS 13:5

We have so much. We have education, food, shelter, knowledge, tech-nology, opportunities, access, abilities, and talents. But still, for reasons carved deep into the walls of our hearts, we want more, better, faster. We glorify a chronic breakneck pace, always moving forward, always upgrading, adding, and amassing. But what if, even for just a few days, we addressed the perfectionism that produces these ugly feelings? What if we took a good look at the burning holes in our hearts to see what they are really shaped like?

Contentment plays an enormous role in our ability to offer ourselves—and others—grace. What is keeping you from settling into a life of contentment?

Contentment is a practice, and it's worth taking up consistently.

Look at your schedule—not just your calendar, but also at all the endless little things that fill up every moment of your white space. What would happen if you just . . . didn't? (And if the answer is nothing, *then just . . . don't.)*

> Just like the pages in our planners, our lives could use more white space.

When we rid ourselves of excess, we make room for **GOD**.

27

GRACE GIVER

"Just as I have loved you, you should love each other."

—JOHN 13:34 NLT

Grace is "the unmerited favor of God toward humanity." And it's not just for those who share our home. Grace is for all the loved ones we hold near and dear—parents, siblings, best friends, and close coworkers. Each of these special people in our lives, whether children or family members or peers, is flawed. They are imperfect, fallible humans. Just like us! And as God pours His unwavering, undeserved grace on us, it's our job to have grace with one another. I really believe that His well is deep and wide and full of the good stuff necessary for acting in grace.

Who could you have more grace with in your life? How can you love him or her, even when it's difficult?

_____

_____

_____

_____

_____

_____

_____

_____

_____

_____

_____

_____

> The grace giver is patient, forgiving, and overflowing with love.

Delivering grace says more about
the deliverer than the recipient.

List three people close to you and ways you can offer them grace.

28

GRACE IN LOVE

Be completely humble and gentle; be patient,
bearing with one another in love.

—EPHESIANS 4:2

If we love our spouses so much, why is it so easy to snap at them? Perhaps it's simply because, after a while, we can take each other for granted and hold each other to higher standards than we hold ourselves.

Having grace with your person is hard sometimes, whether your person is your spouse, a family member, or a best friend. But intentionally pouring love into that person and allowing a standard of grace in your relationship goes a long way.

How can you give more grace to your person?

- **START WITH YOURSELF.** Happiness breeds happiness. If you've embraced your own imperfections, you'll be able to embrace your spouse's imperfections. No one's perfect.
- **NEXT, BE SPECIFIC.** If you're upset about something, name it. Don't mix up the fact that he didn't empty the dishwasher with his worth as a person.
- **AND LASTLY, BE A LOVER.** Okay, now before you start thinking rose petals and candlelight, consider this: a lover is defined as "someone who loves." Don't be so busy with work and life and stuff that you forget to be a lover.

Are you holding your person to a higher standard than you hold yourself? How can you choose to give grace?

Are you a lover? List some ways you can intentionally pour love into your person.

KEEP DATING,
EVEN AFTER
YOU'RE MARRIED.

29

MAKER OF MEMORIES

Love never fails.

—1 CORINTHIANS 13:8

One of the most important things someone once told me about marriage is this: you are responsible for the way you'll look back on your life when you're eighty years old. You're in control of the way you'll feel that day in your rocking chair on your front porch. And you are also responsible for the way your spouse will feel. That's a big deal. Wrap your marriage in love and laughter . . . and lots of grace.

What sort of rocking-chair memories do you want to one day have? What sort of memories do you want for your person?

Make memories
that will be talked
about on rocking
chairs one day.

Marriage is
a lifelong
courtship.

List the things you can do today—in this season of life—to make tomorrow's rocking-chair memories today's reality.

30

GIVE IN TO THE MESS

*Children are a blessing
and a gift from the LORD.*

—PSALM 127:3 CEV

Our time with little ones is so fleeting. It's both the fastest and slowest time of our lives. And for many of us, beginning motherhood coincides with a lot of other important life milestones. Our careers may be taking off. Our parents are getting older. We have big responsibilities and our minds are consumed with bills, to-do lists, behavior issues, comparisons, and attempts at doing everything just right. All the while, our little ones are growing another quarter of an inch. Their chubby thighs are slimming. Their wobbly walks are steadying.

So give in to the mess. Let the craziness win. Consider it giving yourself grace.

My friend Rachel Shingleton once said, "We're all juggling a lot of balls in the air. And when things get hectic, sometimes something has to give. You can drop any of those balls. But you can't drop family." Does your life reflect these words?

The days are
long, but the
years are short.
—GRETCHEN RUBIN

Email, laundry, groceries, and errands can wait another day. What are the things in your life that you're not willing to let wait another day?

There's something wild and freeing about just letting all the balls drop and grabbing on to the one thing that matters.

2016

2015

2014

2013

2012

2011

It's just in our nature to keep going and going. But what if you didn't? What would today look like if you chose the kiddos over the kudos?

31

MODELING GRACE

Train up a child in the way he should go,
And when he is old he will not depart from it.

—PROVERBS 22:6 NKJV

Although parenting is full of sweet, special moments, it's also full of difficult, challenging ones. And there are times when the craziness and sassiness can threaten to push us over the edge into impatience and lost tempers. That's when we need to stop and remember how much those little sponges of ours pick up. Because our kids are learning even when we don't think they are. And they are going to mimic our attitudes, for better or worse. Giving our kids heaping helpings of grace is one of the most special gifts we can give them.

Think back to some of your most challenging parenting (or just people)
moments. How could you better model grace in those moments?

Open your heart to receive God's enormous grace so you can then pour that love and grace on those you love.

In addition to giving your children grace, how might letting them see you give yourself grace change the way they treat themselves—and others?

32

GRACE FOR THE GUILT

Above all, love each other deeply, because
love covers over a multitude of sins.

—1 PETER 4:8

Mommy guilt. It's an epidemic. The working mom, the part-time working mom, the stay-at-home mom, the supermom, the room mom, the traditional mom, the modern mom, the helicopter mom, the tiger mom—no one is immune when mommy guilt rears its ugly head to whisper the lie that we're somehow failing our children. We prioritize and say yes to the right things and no to the wrong things. We do the best we can to be the best moms we can be. And still, mommy guilt lives on.

Mommy guilt is a liar. What lies does it whisper to you?

God does not want
us to beat ourselves
up because we
desperately
want to take a
shower alone.

Now, what is the truth? Here's a handy quiz to tell you definitively if you're doing a good job:

1. Do you love your children?
2. Do you make loving and caring for your people a priority?
3. Are you making the best decisions you can for your family?

If you answered yes to those questions, congratulations! You are a good mom! In fact, you are a great mom. You're doing it, sister!

Tell mommy guilt to take a seat.

Nobody's got time for that nonsense.

33

HANGING UP YOUR CAPE

Am I now trying to win the approval of human beings, or of God?

—GALATIANS 1:10

Is it time for forgive yourself for not being Superwoman?

You don't have to be the best at everything. There is nothing wrong with stepping aside for sanity's sake and allowing someone else to take a leading role. Instead of stretching yourself too thin, create margin and manage your expectations about what you can handle right now. Once you stop beating yourself up for what you're not doing, you're able to be more gracious with the people you love. And you give someone else the chance to shine in the role you couldn't take on. It's okay to hang up your cape.

Is it time to hang up your cape? Are there things that you can step away from so that someone else is able to shine?

_____

_____

_____

_____

_____

_____

_____

_____

_____

Give yourself grace to do what you can, where you are, with what you have.

_____

_____

God created billions of other amazing people with gifts and callings; you don't have to carry the entire weight of the world on your own.

Admitting you can't do it all doesn't mean you have to completely miss out. If you can't find time to serve at the homeless shelter, buy dinner for a family in need instead. Do you wish you could serve more in your church? Pray for your church leaders. List the things you wish you could do. Then, next to each one, list the next best thing you can do.

THE MYTH OF MULTITASKING

Better one handful with tranquillity
than two handfuls with toil
and chasing after the wind.

—ECCLESIASTES 4:6

When we multitask, we think we're accomplishing two things at once. But honestly, can we ever successfully multitask? I don't believe multitasking exists. We're either doing one thing or another, constantly shifting our focus back and forth. In reality, trying to do it all always ends up in robbing one activity or task of your attention so you can give it to the others. It can feel like we're all bustling around as busy as bees, waiting for someone to tell us it's okay to sit down. So here it is: Free your hands. Lock the phone in a drawer. Everything else can wait.

We're all after the elusive state of balance in our lives, whatever that is. How do you define balance? Does multitasking really help you achieve it?

When we multitask our way through the sweetest parts of life, we miss the tiniest joys hidden in the moments between the grand accomplishments.

Yes, there are moments when multitasking seems to work, moments of peace when we think, I've got this! *But how long does that last really?*

We often forget just how much
our overcrowded mental space
contributes to our daily overwhelm.

Just for today, don't multitask. Give you full attention to the thing at hand. Do you feel the difference? What does it feel like?

THE GRACE TO BREATHE

Trust in the LORD with all your heart,
And lean not on your own understanding;
In all your ways acknowledge Him,
And He shall direct your paths.

—PROVERBS 3:5–6 NKJV

Perhaps it's that middle-of-the-night snuggle with a sleeping infant, or perhaps it's watching your child encourage another just the way you've so often encouraged him—God uses these small moments of contentment and success to give us a tiny bit of confidence wrapped in a deep breath for the next time we need it. That's His grace. That's God giving us just what we need to keep going even though we're far from perfect. We live too many days uncertain of the decisions we're making. But in those moments, He assures us that all the little choices we've made were for the right reasons.

Those moments of perfect success and contentment are fleeting. Capture them before they escape. Begin a list here of those grace-filled moments.

> Sometimes, when we're still, when we're right where we need to be, God speaks loud and clear.

How can those moments of sweet perfection sustain you through the not-so-perfect moments and shoot down the lies of mommy guilt?

CELEBRATE THE VICTORIES

The L*ORD* *your God wins victory after victory and is*
always with you. He celebrates and sings because of
you, and he will refresh your life with his love.

—ZEPHANIAH 3:17 CEV

God is in the details. In the small victories, the tiny milestones, the little achievements. Shouldn't we celebrate those things more often than we dwell on the hard stuff or the insecurities? How do we refocus? By taking time to record the little victories. Prayers answered. Moments of peace. Simple solutions. Grateful thoughts. Fill up all the lines on the page. You're training your brain to cultivate confidence and discover hidden happiness, so think differently. Think outside the obvious, and delve into the nooks and crannies of your life. You will be surprised what you discover.

Make a list of this week's victories—no matter how small. Beside each one, name a way to celebrate that victory. Big ways. Small ways. Each-and-every-day ways.

> Gratitude opens the door to God's grace.

Looking at your list of victories, how do you see God meeting you, cheering you on in them? What does that tell you about God?

You're doing
a good job.
Keep going!

God's grace is all around us
if we choose to see it.

37

THE GRACE OF FRIENDSHIP

The heartfelt counsel of a friend
is as sweet as perfume.

—PROVERBS 27:9 NLT

It's easy to feel alone when you're in the thick of it—to feel like no one else in the world understands the battles you fight or the life you live. But this idea—that no one else can relate—can keep us from living in community and from feeling understood and connected. We're all dealing with so many hang-ups when it comes to community. We're worried we won't be accepted if we try to connect. Sometimes it feels easier to be alone and to stick to what we know. But as much as we like to think we can go it alone, we need the grace of friendship.

Are you trying to go it alone? What worries and fears keep you from reaching out and making friends?

God wants friendship for us. He wants us to feel understood and heard. He wants us to have the joy that comes with real face time.

How is friendship a bit of grace you can give yourself?

38

HONEST FRIENDSHIP

A friend loves at all times.

—PROVERBS 17:17

We all buy in to the lie that other women, especially the ones we admire, have it all together. We're afraid to risk being honest about our own imperfections and struggles. And that keeps us from feeling the love and warmth of community—the close community God deeply desires for us. Honest friendships won't be found in gossip or complaining or comparing. It's only when we allow ourselves to be totally imperfect in front of strangers that we find real, genuine friendships.

Who is your ideal friend? Is it someone who's perfect? Or is it someone who is willing to admit she's doesn't have it all together? Why?

> Sincerity levels the playing field and puts us all right where we should be: in the same boat.

Does this view of an ideal friend change the way you present yourself to potential new friends? Are you more willing to risk honesty? To give grace?

_____

_____

_____

_____

It's in sharing the common struggles that we get closer to those around us as we open ourselves up to the empathy, laughs, and understanding that come with saying, "It happens to me too."

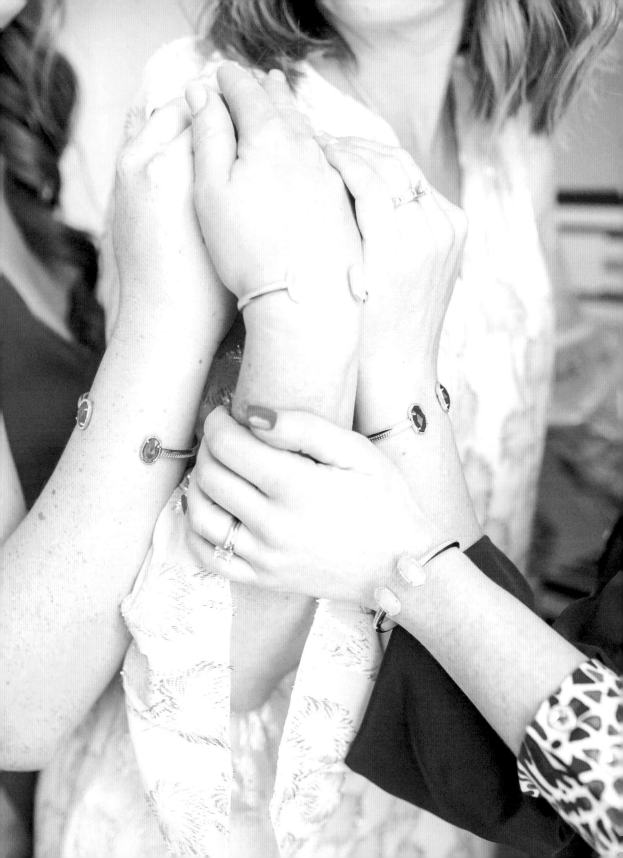

BUILDING A VILLAGE

Two are better than one....
If either of them falls down,
one can help the other up.
But pity anyone who falls
and has no one to help them up.

—ECCLESIASTES 4:9–10

Do you ever feel like that freshman in knee-highs, glancing from her lunch tray to a room of full tables, trying to find a seat? We all want a seat at the table, but we're waiting for someone to stand up, wave us over, and invite us in. In the age of everything fast-paced and high-speed, it's still up to us to create community the old-fashioned way. It takes awkward encounters, continually showing up, and putting ourselves out there.

We all need people in our lives who will encourage us, challenge us, and just show up for us. That's what people in villages do. They care deeply for one another. So build your own village. Invite people to share your table.

Do you need to remind yourself that you're not that freshman in knee-highs anymore? You are God's beloved, grace-given child. Does knowing that give you the courage to invite others to your table?

> Friendship and community are so much about just showing up.

Make a plan to carve out space for friendship. Be specific about when you want to gather and how you can make it happen.

What does it mean to "show up"? Who does this for you? And how can you do it for your village?

40

LOVE UNABASHEDLY

Love one another, for love is of God.

—1 JOHN 4:7 NKJV

Love your people. Love them with big, unapologetic, awkward, whole-hearted love. Because when we feel loved and included, we are accepting of others—good for good. When we are thirsty for approval, we don't use kind or affirming words with others—bad for bad. And when we're over-whelmed, we misplace our anxiety and put blame on the ones we love. Even worse. It's a round-robin, chicken-and-egg situation.

So what if we unabashedly poured love on our loved ones and our communities, even when we don't feel like it? I don't know about you, but when I love, my heart suddenly feels fuller. There is more of me to pour out. What a beautiful circle that is.

What holds you back from loving your people—spouse, children, family, friends,
and even strangers—like there's no tomorrow?

> Give the hugs. Be
> an includer. Let
> everyone have a
> seat at the table.

What if you took the risk? What if you truly loved on the people in your life?
Might if fill up that well inside you? Inside them?

Love others like the
One who loves you.

41

THE GRACE OF REST

"Come with me by yourselves to a quiet place and get some rest."

—MARK 6:31

Rest recharges our bodies and refreshes our souls. As a society, we've lost the ability to be still in our minds. We take our phones to bed with us and find every reason in the world to fill our hands and minds with stuff. Practice the art of stillness without distraction. Stop checking your phone at red lights or multitasking during times with the ones you love. Sit, stare out the window, and sing along with the radio. Simple is an opportunity to refresh. So rest. Be still. Let your tank fill itself while your body refuels.

Sleep is the most obvious form of rest, but some seasons of life allow for little sleep. What are other ways you find rest?

When we pare down life to its simplest, most beautifully basic parts, we're left with room to enjoy each other, to rest, and to truly savor life with all our hearts, minds, and spirits.

How would taking time to rest—both the waking and the sleeping kind—change your routine, your outlook, your ability to roll with the punches of this life?

Finding rest is as much about simplifying as it is about changing the attitude of your heart.

42

A PERSPECTIVE OF GRACE

I will praise you, LORD, with all my heart;
I will tell of all the marvelous things you have done.

—PSALM 9:1 NLT

Perspective is everything. God guides our hearts to focus on one aspect of a situation for a bit and then refocus on another. It's like using a camera lens—and God gives us the ability to operate the camera. That focus shapes our attitude and ultimately impacts our people in immeasurable ways.

Yes, God may have you in waiting or may have pulled you through a tragedy, but the camera is yours. You control your perspective and the state of your heart in the situation you are in today—even when you can't control the circumstances. Choose gratitude and grace every morning.

Gratitude and grace go hand in hand. So what are you grateful for? Big and small, make a list.

> "It is not joy that makes us grateful; it is gratitude that makes us joyful."
>
> —BROTHER DAVID STEINDL-RAST

Consider making a photo wall of the moments you're most grateful for. What moments would you have represented there? If you don't have photos of them, what objects might remind you of the gratefulness you felt?

Grace and gratitude go hand in hand.

43

GRACE IN THE GIGGLES

A cheerful heart is good medicine.

—PROVERBS 17:22

We all have a tendency to take life too seriously. We overcomplicate, over-think, and overcommit. Sometimes I think we're all just hamster-wheeling this whole crazy gift of life right out from under our feet. When I feel lost and like I'm spinning out of control on my little wheel, sometimes all I can do is laugh. A good laugh at just the right moment can make the ridicu-lousness of my plans, worries, and anxieties fall away. Sometimes God's grace is in the giggles.

How can shared laughter help turn down the tension, tame the anxiety, and help remind you of all you have to be grateful for?

What better way
to have grace with
ourselves and our
people than to laugh
and let go when life
gets too uptight?

Whether it's over a glass of spilled milk or a heartbreaking diagnosis, how can shared laughter be a gift of grace?

The importance of
gratitude is followed
closely by the
importance of having
a sense of humor.

GOD MEETS US WITH GRACE

Those who hope in the LORD will renew their strength.
They will soar on wings like eagles; they will run and
not grow weary, they will walk and not be faint.

—ISAIAH 40:31

Sweet sister, are you weary? Then hear this truth: God will fill your cup and give you strength when you physically can't do it. He will give you grace—so that you, in turn, can give grace in the way you serve and love your people. Because God's way of revealing Himself to us is by revealing Himself *in* us.

When we show God's love and grace, we are living, breathing examples of His perfect love. God will meet you where you are—wherever you are. Because He desperately wants us to spread His big, unabashed love all over the place.

When the mess—whether it's the house, the money, the diagnosis—threatens to overwhelm, how can you show the love and grace of God to your people through your own gift of grace?

List three ways you can spread God's big, unabashed love all over your place today.

God meets us in our mess to connect us,
strengthen us, and grow our gratitude.

45

GRACE IN YOUR CALLING

For we are God's handiwork, created in Christ Jesus to do
good works, which God prepared in advance for us to do.

—EPHESIANS 2:10

God designed each of us with a specific purpose in mind. For some, it's to invest our time and hearts fully into motherhood. For others, it's to manage businesses that contribute to the greater good of our world. Some were designed to teach and nurture others. Whatever your calling is, it is of great importance, and God wrote it on your heart when He made you. It can take time to discover, and it can change over the course of your life. Whatever God created you to do, He lit a tiny, flickering flame in you that's just waiting to be discovered and fanned.

Whatever you can write, sing, or talk about for hours—that is the calling God's leading you to. What is God calling you to in this season for your life?

Everyone has
a calling.

List some steps you can take to start fanning the flame God has lit within you.

God would not fill your heart with a calling without

also filling your spirit with all you need to answer it.

46

THE LIFE YOU DREAM OF

*Now to him who is able to do immeasurably more
than all we ask or imagine, according to his power
that is at work within us, to him be glory.*

—EPHESIANS 3:20–21

We talk so much about choosing jobs or selecting careers. But what if we chose a life instead? Whether you're seventeen or seventy-five, you can define the life you want to have. Better yet, you can decide how you want to spend your days. God numbered and gave you every single one of those days, so what if you lived each one to its absolute fullest?

You, my friend, have options. Design a life that is beautiful and filling and impactful. Yes, it takes hard work, sacrifice, and planning, but it is possible to create the life you dream of.

Define the life you dream of having. What words spring to mind?

Your job is just
one tiny part
of your life.

Don't hold yourself back when imagining the future you want. What stepping stones can you place on the path now to create the life you dream of? What can you do tomorrow? And the next day? Make a list. Make a plan. Do it.

Run like crazy down the path God has set your heart ablaze for, and the One who loves you will be around every corner, cheering you on.

47

IT'S OKAY TO GET DIRTY

*"Keep on seeking, and you will find. Keep on
knocking, and the door will be opened to you."*

—LUKE 11:9 NLT

No matter what your passions are in this life or what road you're traveling
or what goal you're chasing, know this: it's okay to get dirty. It's okay to try
one thing, mess up, and try something else. It's also okay to keep trying
to climb that same tree, even if you fall down ten times. The difference
between people who achieve their goals and people who don't is their
ability to dust themselves off and wear their dirty outfit proudly.

Who are the people you admire? In business? In relationships? Are they afraid to get dirty, or do they wear their dirty outfit proudly?

Go and do
and be all the
things you
want to be.

GIVE YOURSELF
THE GRACE TO BE YOU.

So what are you afraid of? What would it look like to step into a perfectly imperfect life that you are truly passionate about? Can you give yourself the permission—and the grace—to reach out for real joy?

GRACE-FULL RECOVERY

"I have prayed for you, that your faith should not fail."

—LUKE 22:32 NKJV

The truth is, we all fall down. We all mess up and make mistakes and do and say the wrong things sometimes. But the beauty is in the recovery. It's in the way you handle yourself as you pick up the pieces. It's in having dignity when you're embarrassed. It's in being grateful when you're exhausted. It's in having integrity when you've made a mistake. No matter what path you're on, you know what I'm talking about—you know the pain of face-planting and the embarrassment that comes when you just can't meet expectations. These situations aren't always negatives. Instead, they're often opportunities for us to show what we're truly made of.

Think of the times you've fallen, messed up, and just plain face-planted. How did you handle the recovery?

Dare to live days
that fill you instead
of drain you—
even if that means
giving yourself a
little extra grace.

How can you show yourself grace in those times? Are you better able then to show grace to others when they fall?

Choose to do things with heart.

STEPPING OUT IN GRACE

Let all who take refuge in you be glad;
let them ever sing for joy.
Spread your protection over them,
that those who love your name may rejoice in you.

—PSALM 5:11

Your desire for a better life has to be stronger than your fear of what it may take to get there. It's as simple as that. Don't put off creating the life you dream of because you're afraid you can't do it perfectly. If you're waiting on the clouds to part and pretty rainbows to mark each step, you're going to be waiting a while. Today is the day. That beautifully bumpy road is just waiting for you to take your first step. You were made for this! You will make mistakes. You will fall down. It might hurt, but it makes life so much better than before.

God is constantly growing us, constantly pruning us, constantly pushing us. But do you see how His efforts will ultimately lead you to the life of your dreams?

_____

_____

_____

_____

_____

_____

_____

_____

_____

_____

_____

_____

_____

_____

Is fear holding you back from pursuing your dream? Surrender those fears to God here—and ask Him to show you the next step to take on your journey.

God can perfectly orchestrate every failure and milestone into a song of daily surrender and joy.

A BEAUTIFUL PLAN

"I know the plans I have for you," declares the
Lord, "plans to prosper you and not to harm you,
plans to give you hope and a future."

—JEREMIAH 29:11

This isn't how it was supposed to look . . .

Stop right there. How is it supposed to look? When we create fantasy images in our heads, we slay the beauty in our lives. Comparison truly is the thief of joy. And we've established that standard of perfection in our work and our families based on what? Social media highlight reels? "Perfect" people? God has a way of making our seasons make sense. Sometimes it just takes a little bit of leaning in to realize that even if life doesn't look as glamorous as it could, His beautiful plan is still at work.

What if your beautiful mess is all part of God's beautiful plan? Does that thought change the way you see not only the mess, but yourself and your role in the lives of your people?

_____

_____

_____

_____

_____

Love with real love, not styled love.

_____

_____

_____

_____

_____

_____

How can you not only give yourself grace in the midst of the mess but allow
yourself to also find joy and fulfillment?

Let some things
slide. It's okay.

Embrace the
season you are
in by leaning in
and loving big.

A LEGACY OF GRACE

Follow the example of Christ.

—1 JOHN 2:6 CEV

One day we'll add up all our seasons—the joyous ones, the heart-wrenching ones, the momentous, average, and peaceful ones. When we do, we'll have one rich life story. An illustration of faith and doubt, grace and worry, friendship, learning, and loving. Each season connects to the next with links of growth and change. We'll each look back at that chain of experiences with meaningful stories to tell. We'll unpack nuggets of goodness and pass on hard-earned wisdom. Sure, we may have scars from the countless times we bit it, but we'll be really good at standing back up. That, friends, is what legacy is.

Putting away the perfectionism, the comparisons, the styled-life expectations, what do you want your real legacy to be? Love? Grace? Friendship? A life with white space?

Walk intentionally through this life and don't just skip along the path blindly.

The gift of your legacy is what you are giving your people today. What does that knowledge motivate you to do? To not do?

God's grace is all around you, settling on and highlighting the little joys and tiny blessings you may not always see.

THE JOURNEY OF GRACE

For it is by grace you have been saved, through faith—
and this is not from yourselves, it is the gift of God.

—EPHESIANS 2:8

Right now, in this moment, you have the opportunity to welcome God's grace into your life. Now is your chance to tell yourself the truth: You are measuring up. You are doing a good job. You, just as you are, are enough.

Be still, sweet girl. Listen. Let God's truth resonate in your life just as it is. Not one day when your house is clean. Not when all the laundry is put away. Not when the time is right. But right now. The joy is found in the journey—a journey of simple and profound grace poured constantly on perfectly imperfect women like you and me.

What are the truths you want—need—to tell yourself? The ones you most want to remember when the craziness gets crazier and the journey seems endless?

You are enough. Enough for yourself. Enough for God. And enough for the ones you love.

Sit, palms up, with your eyes closed. Listen. What story will you live? It's totally up to you. Is it a story of grace? Trust? Faith? Growth? Choose your next step.

When God strips us of all the things that make us feel safe and secure, He gives us a story far better than we could have written for ourselves.

GOD'S GRACE IS
ALL AROUND YOU.
SEE IT.
EMBRACE IT.
SHARE IT.

OVERCOMING OVERWHELM

Thank you so much for purchasing this exclusive Target® edition of *A Standard of Grace*. As a busy mama to three, a businesswoman, a wife, and so much more, I understand the circus life can be—because I'm living it alongside you. God desires so much more for us than chasing to-do lists and struggling to keep up. I hope this book has filled and inspired a little part of your heart and encouraged you to hold yourself to a standard of grace every day.

xo,

emily

CONTENTS

I JUST CAN'T KEEP UP.

Q I've washed the same load of laundry three times this week. My schedule couldn't be more packed. My inbox is exploding. Everyone needs my attention. Now what?

A That feeling—that there is an elephant on your chest and you can't breathe? You control it. Sometimes the simplest thing you can do when life is anything but simple is lean in. Give yourself the grace of five minutes. Sit and count your breaths amongst the mess of it all. Whatever it is, it can wait. Just sit and be still. Gather your thoughts and start task one.

MY HOME IS SO MESSY THAT I CAN'T THINK STRAIGHT.

Q When I'm at home, all I can think about is how much I need to do, buy, organize, and throw away. Where do I even begin?

A Your home should be a place of love, comfort, and joy—not necessarily a place of total order and Pinterest-perfect organization. Start by making the rounds with a trash bag. Next, throw everything that's out of place in a laundry basket. Then work on putting away what's in the basket. Now, circle your house with a donate bag. Remember, your home shouldn't feel magazine perfect. It should make you happy and help you live a good life.

I'M STUCK, LOST, AND EMPTY.

Q   I care for my people really well. I make sure they have everything they need and a lot of love and joy in their lives. But when it comes to me, I'm running on empty.

A   When we feel like we've dished out all the love we have and are left feeling ragged, it's because our wells are empty. It's up to you to fill your well even when there's not another minute of time left for you. Make time. Make yourself a priority. Even if all you can do is walk outside for two minutes for fresh air, do it. You give out what you put in. If you run in Captain Mode too long, you'll crash and burn. Light a candle. Take a walk. Eat the chocolate. Go to bed early. Read a book. Fill your well. You matter too.

I CAN'T GET EVERYTHING DONE.

Q How do I get important things done without sacrificing the good stuff like sleep or family time?

A When your to-do list starts to run you instead of you managing it, it's time to take a step back. Though everything might look like number-one priority, there is absolutely an order to those tasks. Be realistic about what has to get done and what can wait a day or two. Done is better than perfect. Move things along, but don't sacrifice the good. Half an unfinished task list is so much better than a full list of regrets.

MY MIND WON'T STOP SPINNING.

Q I'm overwhelmed by so many things spinning in my mind day in and day out. How do I quiet my thoughts?

A This is the exact reason why I created the Simplified® Planner. I had a hard time focusing on what mattered most when my mind was crammed full of lists, reminders, tasks, thoughts, worries, and ideas. The best way to wrangle all these things is to find a place to put them. Get them out of your head. Whether you find a planner, a notebook, an app, or a napkin, write down everything in your head. Download it all, and make space for peace, calm, and rest. Brain space is everything.

I CAN'T KEEP UP WITH MY KIDS.

Q   My kids undo everything I do all day long. I love them to pieces, but I have to do things over and over. I feel so task-oriented and I want to be people-oriented.

A   You're speaking my language here. Letting go is hard. In my experience, with three active little ones, it's best to let the house be a mess during the day. I clean up the highchairs after every meal, but I don't sweep the floor. I do what needs to be done to get to the next phase of the day, but I let the rest go until after bedtime. That way, we start each day fresh and don't spin our wheels all day long. Do what matters. Forget the rest.

I'M STRETCHED TERRIBLY THIN.

Q   I've said yes to everyone and everything. I'm stretched so thin that I don't have time for what I truly love. I thought I was doing well by serving others, but now I'm good for no one.

A   Today is the day you start saying no to any- and everything that isn't absolutely necessary. No, you cannot serve on that committee because it will take time away from your family. No, you cannot have another play date because you need some one-on-one time at home. No, you cannot meet for coffee because right now you need some mental space. Say no. Free up space to feel creative, to breathe, and to love. It's okay to slow down. The world won't forget you. You won't miss out. In fact, you may find true joy waiting in what you now have time for.